Y0-DDR-055

PEOPLE AT WORK

Bobbie Kalman
Susan Hughes

The In My World Series

BEACH SCHOOL LIBRARY
1710 N. HUMBOLDT
PORTLAND, OREGON 97217

ECIA CHAPTER II
Property Of
Portland, School District

Toronto
New York Crabtree Publishing Company

The In My World Series
Created by Bobbie Kalman

Writing team:
Bobbie Kalman
Susan Hughes

Editor-in-Chief:
Bobbie Kalman

Editors:
Rachel Atlas
Susan Hughes
Lise Gunby

Cover and title page design:
Oksana Ruczenczyn, Leslie Smart and Associates

Design and mechanicals:
Catherine Johnston
Nancy Cook

Illustrations:
Title page by Karen Harrison
Pages 28-31 by VictoR Gad
© Crabtree Publishing Company 1985, 1986
Pages 4-27 and cover © Mitchell Beazley Publishers 1982

Copyright © 1986 Crabtree Publishing Company
All rights reserved. No part of this publication may
be reproduced, stored in a retrieval system, or be
transmitted in any form or by any means, electronic,
mechanical, photocopying, recording, or otherwise,
without the prior written permission of Crabtree
Publishing Company.

Cataloging in Publication Data

Kalman, Bobbie, 1947–
    People at work

(The In my world series)
ISBN 0-86505-068-6 (bound) –
ISBN 0-86505-090-2 (pbk.)

1. Work – Juvenile literature. 2. Occupations –
Juvenile literature. I. Hughes, Susan, 1960–
II. Title. III. Series.

HD4902.5.K34   1986   j331.7'02

To Scott and Heather

350 Fifth Avenue
Suite 3308
New York, N.Y. 10118

102 Torbrick Road
Toronto, Ontario
Canada M4J 4Z5

Contents

A world of jobs

People all over the world are working. In the country, they wake up at dawn to do the chores on the farm. In the cities and towns, they hurry to offices and factories early in the morning. People in this city picture are going to work. A busy day lies ahead!

People do many kinds of jobs. You can see some of them in this picture. There are bus drivers and train drivers. An architect is hard at work in his office. There are people selling newspapers and sweeping the streets. Many people have just arrived for work on the subways and buses. What types of jobs might they be going to?

People usually earn money for the work they do. They use the money to buy things, such as books or food, that other people have worked to make. They use the money to buy the services of other working people such as actors or lawyers.

Every job is important, and every job is different. What kind of job would you like to have? Perhaps you will be a hair stylist or an accountant. You could be an airplane pilot or a dentist. You could be a singer in a rock band, a football player, or a veterinarian!

Picture talk

What kind of jobs do you enjoy doing?
How do you feel when you've done a job well?
Can you name a job for each letter of the alphabet?

Fixing our car

Our car is a lemon. That's what my mom says, anyway. She says a lemon is a car that always needs repairs. It won't work properly.

I'm glad that our car is a lemon. That means we have to take it to the garage at least once a month! I love going to the garage. When we arrived at the garage today, the mechanic came right over and said to my dad and me, "Hello Mr. McNair. Hello Ian. What's the problem this time?"

My dad said, "Hello Mr. Sanchez. I can't say that I'm happy to see you!" We all laughed. We have been friends for a long time. We've been friends ever since we bought our lemon.

Mr. Sanchez lifted the hood of the car. "Ah yes," he said quickly. "Here's the problem." He took out the air filter. "You need a new one of these," he said. Mr. Sanchez is a good *mechanic*. He knows all about the insides of cars, just as our doctor knows about the insides of our bodies. Mr. Sanchez knows how all the parts of the engine fit together. He knows how to use his tools to fix or replace parts.

Soon Mr. Sanchez said, "All set!" My dad paid him and said, "Thanks. See you next month." We all laughed. What a lemon of a car!

Picture talk

Why is one mechanic wearing a mask?
Why do you think one of the customers looks unhappy?

Doctors, nurses, and volunteers

"Good-bye," Anne says. She waves to me. "Good-bye Anne," I call. I can't wave to her because I am holding on to my crutches. I broke my leg when I was learning to ski.

The doctor put a cast on my leg. I would like to be able to do her job! She told me that it takes many years of studying at school and in the hospital to become a doctor. It must be very hard to learn about all those medicines and treatments. I like the doctor. She has gentle hands and wears her hair in a bun. I like the nurses here, too. Nurse Ellen is helping me to walk with my crutches.

I had my leg X-rayed in the X-ray room. Now I am on the children's floor. It is a busy place! Many people work here, but they are not all experts in medicine. Some of them are here to make people feel better in other ways! These people are called *volunteers*. They do not get paid. They come to the hospital to cheer up the patients. They read and talk to them, or bring them their meals. The doctors and nurses are happy for the help!

I am sorry I broke my leg, but being in the hospital was fun. When I am old enough, maybe I will be a volunteer. I might even be a nurse or a doctor!

Picture talk

What jobs can you see being done in the picture?
Would you like to work in a hospital? What job would you do?

9

Our music teacher

Rat-a-tat-tat. Rat-a-tat-tat. I am playing the drum. I watch Mr. Frazier's hands. When he points at me, I know it is the signal for me to begin my drum roll.

Mr. Frazier is our music teacher. He spent many years in school learning how to play music. Then he went to teacher's college to learn how to be a music teacher. It's funny to think that teachers teach people to teach!

Mr. Frazier says that learning to play an instrument well is hard work and takes a long time. When we first began our music classes, we all sounded terrible. We have improved a lot since then. Mr. Frazier says being a good teacher takes a lot of practice, too! He says he's improved since he first began teaching!

Mr. Frazier likes being a teacher. He works at school all week from eight in the morning until four or five in the afternoon. Mr. Frazier says he often stays late in the evening until all his work is done. On Tuesday nights, he takes a course in astronomy. He says he likes to learn about new things. On Thursday nights, he plays trombone with a jazz band. Soon his band will be coming to play at our school. Maybe they can play a song with our music class!

Picture talk

Name the instruments in this picture.
For many people, playing music is a job. Who are your favorite musicians?

BEACH SCHOOL LIBRARY
1710 N. HUMBOLDT
PORTLAND, OREGON 97217

Getting my hair cut

This morning Mom took my sister and me to have our hair cut. I had my hair cut first. Mark was the *stylist*. He used his scissors and a comb. Snip, snip, snip. As he got closer to my ears, I began to worry. What if Mark made a mistake? What if he cut my hair too short? What if he cut all my hair off? What if he cut my ear?

My mother must have seen me looking worried. She came over and whispered to me, "Mark is a very good stylist. He went to a special school to learn how to cut and style hair. He practiced on wigs first and then he practiced on volunteers. When he came to work here, his *supervisor* taught him more about cutting all kinds of hair. Now Mark can even do a good job on hair as long and messy as yours!"

Mom laughed and I smiled. Snip, snip, snip, snip. I opened my comic book. I wasn't worried anymore. Do you think my sister looks worried?

Picture talk

Some of the workers in the shop are *assistants*. They are learning how to cut hair. They must also do other jobs such as sweeping the floor or washing hair. Which workers do you think are assistants?

Stylists must practice on wigs before they can cut customers' hair. Why? Tell a story about a hair stylist who made a mistake.

How is being a hair stylist like being an artist? Look at the photographs on the wall in the picture. Which hair style do you like best?

Working with wood

This is Len's workshop. He is a woodworker. Three men work for him. People who are paid to work for someone are called *employees*. The person who hires them is called an *employer*.

Sam is an *apprentice* woodworker. He is learning woodworking skills from Len. An apprentice does not earn much money because he is a beginner. As he learns more, he will earn more money. He will become a skilled worker.

Len and Sam are building a table. They have made diagrams to help them measure the pieces of wood. They used a saw to cut the boards to the right lengths. Now they are fitting the pieces together.

Mike is building a wooden tricycle. He is using a tool called a *spanner* to attach the wheels and pedals to the tricycle. Mike is an experienced woodworker. He has been working for Len for many years. Len has asked Mike to be his partner. Mike will share the cost of running the shop. He will also get a share of the *profits* or the money that the shop earns.

Picture talk

What mistakes might an apprentice make while he is learning woodworking skills? Woodworkers use their hands to make and fix things. In what other jobs do people work with their hands?

What problems might business partners have? Would you rather be an employer or an employee? Explain your choice.

A family business

Last night our family went to a restaurant. The restaurant is owned by our friends. It is a *family business*. Mr. and Mrs. Xilias and their son, George, are Greek. They work together making and serving Greek food.

We had a wonderful time. I watched Mr. Xilias make shish kebabs. He put pieces of lamb, tomatoes, onions, mushrooms, and green peppers on a skewer. Then he placed the skewer on the grill over the charcoal. Mrs. Xilias took the cooked meat and vegetables off the skewer and put them on plates beside steaming hot rice and a lemony green salad.

George was our waiter. He works part-time in the restaurant. During the day, he takes business courses at a university. He says he is also learning a lot about business right here at the restaurant. When he graduates, George hopes to open a chain of shish-kebab restaurants with his parents. He wants to call them "Kebab Caves." George's father likes the idea, but he wishes George would first learn to get the food to the customers before it gets cold!

Picture talk

What special dish does the Xilias family serve?
What ingredients do they use?
What is George learning at school? What does he hope to do in the future?
Would you like to own a business? Why? Why not? What kind of business would you open?

The best pilot in the world!

My mother has an exciting job. She flies huge planes all over the world. Tonight she is going to Paris, France. She has been sleeping all day so she will be wide-awake when she flies.

My mother loves flying jumbo jets best, but she can remember when she flew tiny planes with only one engine. She started flying when she was just eighteen. Her father was a pilot. He taught her how to fly. My mother has flown thousands of hours since then. She is one of the best pilots in the world! At least, I think so.

There are many people who work with my mother on the plane and at the airport. The *copilots* help my mother to fly the plane. The *flight attendants* serve food and drinks to the passengers. *Air-traffic controllers* work hard in the airport control tower. They can see every plane on their *radar screens*. This helps them to organize the airplane traffic! They make sure my mother and other pilots take off and land safely.

One of the best things about having a pilot for a mother is that three times a year we get passes to travel anywhere in the world by plane. We have been to Europe, Japan, Australia, and even the Fiji Islands!

Picture talk

Would you like to be a pilot? Why? Why not?
What jobs do people at this airport do?
What job would you like to do at this airport?
Have you ever gone anywhere by plane?
Where?

Office workers

This is the office of a toy company. The company hires many employees. Everyone must cooperate and work together to run a big business like this one.

There are many different kinds of jobs done in this office. *Salespeople* sell the toys to stores. They both visit stores and work in the office.

Accountants keep track of the money that the company spends making the toys and that it earns selling the toys.

The *secretaries* help the office to run smoothly. They type reports and letters. They use the computer to store information.

Managers are in charge of the business. They make important decisions about buying and selling. They plan for the future of the company. They decide how many employees the company should hire.

Bradley used to be a *clerk*. He took courses at night. Now he is a salesperson. Many people become interested in new things. People often change jobs several times.

Picture talk

Name and describe all the tools or equipment these people are using.

Point to each person in the picture and say what job you think he or she does. Explain your reasons.

Which of these jobs would you choose? Why?

Working in a factory

This is a factory where cars are made. Each employee works one *shift* of eight hours a day. A shift is the period of time that a group works. The day shift is from 7 o'clock in the morning to 3 o'clock in the afternoon. The evening shift is from 3 o'clock in the afternoon to 11 o'clock at night. The night shift is from 11 o'clock at night until 7 o'clock in the morning. The factory is busy every hour of the day.

These cars are being built on an *assembly line*. Workers stand along a line of machinery. Different people add different parts to the cars. Some workers are in charge of putting on wheels. Some work the painting machine. All of the workers cooperate to *assemble* or put together the cars.

Can you see the beginning of this assembly line? Huge presses shape flat pieces of steel into car parts. There are side panels, doors, and roofs. The pieces are clamped and welded together. The frame is dipped in a liquid that will stop the car from rusting. The car is painted. Seats, bumpers, lights, and other parts are added. The engine is installed, and tires are put on the car. The gas, oil, and water tanks are filled. The team of workers has now completed another car!

Picture talk

Describe each step in assembling a car. What would happen if the stages in the assembly line got mixed up?

24

My mother, the homemaker

My mother makes our home run smoothly. She is in charge of most of the jobs that have to do with the house and family.

She gets up very early in the morning to change little Marta and feed her. She starts breakfast and puts out the clothes we will wear to school. She reminds Paul and me not to forget our lunches and books. After we leave on the school bus, Mom washes the clothes and hangs them outside to dry. She cleans the house. She plans the meals for the week and goes grocery shopping.

After Paul and I are brought home on the bus, we play outside while Mom takes down the dry washing. Marta lies on a rug under an umbrella which protects her from the hot sun. Soon it will be time for Mom to make dinner. She lets us help with the mixing and measuring!

Mom is the accountant in our home. She pays all the bills. She makes sure the money my dad earns covers all our expenses. Mom patches us up when we are hurt and nurses us when we are sick. She helps us with our homework. There is very little my mother can't do. She even cuts our hair!

Picture talk

Name all the jobs this mother does.
What jobs can her children help her to do?
Some mothers work outside the home. How can all the work in the home get done?

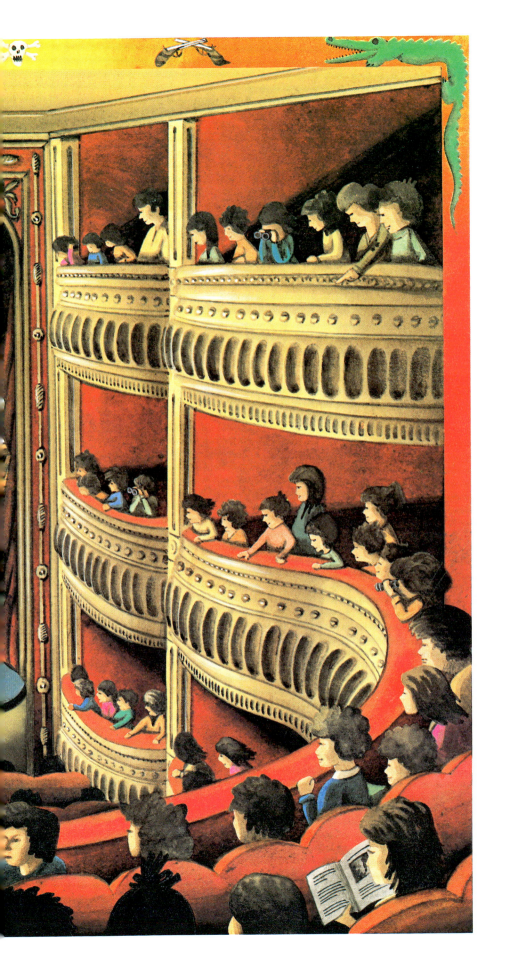

Let's look at the theater

Have you ever been to the theater? Have you ever seen *actors* and *actresses* performing on the stage? They have fun when they act, but they are also working. They have practiced hard to memorize their lines and their movements. They have worked many hours to create their characters for you, the audience!

Many people work *backstage* in a theater. Some are *make-up artists*. They can use wigs and make-up to make a young person look old and an old person look young. *Costume designers* create clothes for the characters in the play. *Set designers* decide how the stage will look. Other workers build *props*, like the boat on the stage in this picture. They look after the lighting and create sound effects.

Every play has a *director*. A director is in charge of the play from start to finish. He gives instructions to the actors and actresses. The *producer* has an important job, too. She looks after the business and makes sure there is enough money to pay people for their hard work!

Picture talk

Look closely at this stage. How do you think the props were made?
Do you prefer movies or theater? Why?
Have you ever acted in a play? Would you like to try acting?
What is your favorite television show?

Let's explore . . . How books are made

My parents are publishers

My name is Samantha. I live in a world of books. Why? My parents own a publishing company! They work hard. Sometimes they work late at night and on weekends. They travel a lot, too. They show their books to people all over the world! My parents started the company a month before I was born. When I was four, I thought every home had typewriters in the living room!

What my dad and Alice do

Let me tell you about the people in my parents' publishing company. My father runs the business part of our company. He is the *publisher*. He figures out how many books should be published each year. He finds people to sell the books. He decides which printing company should print the books. He pays the employees. He is in charge of the money the company earns and spends.

Alice is my dad's *assistant*. She does many jobs for my father, but her biggest job is making sure that the right information goes into the company computer.

The people who work on the books

There are many steps in publishing a set of books. Several people work on each step of the process. I like getting to know all the people in the company. I drop in at the office every day after school and talk to everyone. Sometimes the editors read stories to me to see if I like them. The editors call me their most important *critic*.

My mother is the *editor-in-chief*. She finds out which books librarians, teachers, and parents need. She hires the writers and editors that will help her to create the books.

Susan is a *writer* and *editor*. She and my mother make an *outline* for each book. Susan *researches* the books. She and my mother then start writing. They create stories and poems. They write activities for kids to try. They work hard to make the books fun to read. They check each other's work. Then they type up everything they have written. These typewritten pages are called *manuscripts*.

While the manuscripts are being written, artists, such as Karen and Victor, draw pictures to illustrate the pages. The artists take a long time, but their illustrations are worth the wait! Cathy, our *production coordinator,* keeps everyone working on schedule. She has to make sure the books are published on time.

The journey of the manuscripts

The manuscripts go to Diane. Diane is a teacher. She reads the manuscripts and checks to make sure that kids my age will be able to understand and enjoy the ideas in the manuscripts. Diane suggests how to make the books better.

Now the manuscript goes on to Lise, the *free-lance editor.* Free lance means she works for many publishers. Lise rewrites the parts of the manuscripts that Diane thought needed improvement. She also checks the facts to make sure they are correct. She checks the grammar, spelling, and punctuation.

The manuscripts are now sent out to be *typeset*. The typesetter types the words into a machine which is like a camera. The letters are photographed onto special paper and developed. The sheets of typesetting are called *galley proofs* or galleys. The galleys are read one more time by my mother, Susan, Lise, and sometimes Roger, Rachel, or Dan, who are copy editors and *proofreaders*. They look for mistakes that might still be in the galley proofs—and they always find some!

While this is going on, all the illustrations have been finished. Oksana is designing the covers for the books and my dad is writing the *brochure* which advertises the books. Oksana will then design and finish the brochure.

Now comes my favorite part! Cathy and Nancy do the *paste-up*. They match the galley proofs to the illustrations. Then Cathy runs the galleys through the waxing machine. This puts hot wax on the back of the galleys. Cathy presses the sticky galleys onto sheets of heavy plastic. My mother and the proofreaders read the galleys one last time.

Finally, Cathy takes the pasted-up galleys and illustrations to Arnie. Arnie works for the printing company which is printing our books. He makes sure the printers who work on our books do the very best job they can. After the

books are *printed*, they are *bound*. This means the pages are sewn together and the covers are attached.

Joanne and Spot

The finished books are delivered to our warehouse. Joanne runs the warehouse with our cat, Spot. People who want to buy the books order them from Joanne. She makes sure the books are packaged and sent out by the *shippers*. Spot makes sure no mice get near our books. He keeps watch by running in and out among the boxes. Sometimes he sits on Joanne's desk. He thinks he's the boss.

I like our publishing company. I like all the people who work on the books. But I must confess, Spot is absolutely my favorite employee!

Try this . . . Tidytime Boogie

Jennifer and Jonas did not like helping around the house. They made sure they could not be found when their mother had that "Let's clean the house!" look in her eye.

One day, Jennifer and Jonas went to visit their friends, Maureen and Justin.

Maureen said, "Hi! You're just in time to play a fun game with us. It's called "Tidytime Boogie." It's one of our favorite games."

Jennifer and Jonas said they'd love to play. Maureen's and Justin's mom, Donna, and her boyfriend, Charlie, decided to join in, too.

Maureen and Justin tore a sheet of paper into strips. They wrote one cleaning job on each strip. Some of these jobs were:

vacuuming the carpets
dusting the furniture
waxing the wooden furniture
collecting and putting out the garbage
making the beds
tidying each room
folding the laundry
washing the dishes
drying and putting away the dishes
mopping the kitchen floor
mopping the bathroom floor
cleaning the tub and sink area in the
  bathroom

Donna folded the slips of paper and put them into a hat. Each person chose two slips and read their jobs aloud.

"Is everyone all set?" asked Charlie.

"Hey, wait a minute. This sounds like cleaning!" Jonas complained. "And there is nothing we hate more!"

"Just give it a try. We promise you'll have a great time," urged Justin.

The stereo was turned up LOUD! Music filled all the rooms. Donna danced to the broom closet. She took out the mop, wiggled her hips, and danced the mop around the kitchen floor until the floor sparkled. Charlie leaped to the beat with his spray wax. In the time it took for one song to finish, the furniture shone so brightly, Charlie could see himself in it.

Maureen fluffed the covers as she pirouetted around the beds. She smoothed out the wrinkles in time to the happy beat. Justin vacuumed quickly and practiced his favorite dance steps. Jennifer belted out her favorite song as she wiped the bathtub, and Jonas folded the clean clothes as if he were a musical robot.

Before the second tape was even finished, the house was spotless. The musical cleaning brigade had finished its work. Everyone felt great and no one was tired! They all kept dancing until the tape was finished.

Then Jennifer and Jonas rushed right home and played the game again—this time at *their* home with their parents. Who would have thought cleaning could be so much fun!

Work dictionary

accountant   A person whose job is to keep, manage, and go over records or accounts of money that is received or paid out.

architect   A person who designs and plans buildings or other structures and supervises the construction by the builders.

assembly line   A line of workers and machines. The product being assembled or put together passes from one stage of assembly to the next until it is completed.

astronomy   The study of the stars, planets, and other heavenly bodies.

backstage   In or toward the area of the theater behind the stage.

business   A trade or occupation that is a person's source of income.

career   A person's profession or occupation.

character   A person represented in a play, movie, or novel.

clerk   An office worker whose job is to keep records, accounts, or files. A clerk also does general office work, such as typing.

copy editor   One who proofreads and looks for grammatical or spelling mistakes in a manuscript.

designer   A person who creates designs, such as dress designs or automobile designs.

equipment   A thing or things needed for a particular purpose or use.

expert   A person with special knowledge or skill in a certain area.

factory   A building or a group of buildings where goods are made.

goods   Things that are made to be sold.

jumbo jet   An extremely large airplane that is driven by jet propulsion.

lawyer   A person who is trained to give advice about laws and to represent clients in court.

manuscript   The typewritten or handwritten version of a book, article, or other work.

partner   A person who joins or shares with another or others, especially in a business where profits and losses are shared.

part-time   For only part of the usual working time.

printer   A company which runs printing presses; a person whose business is printing.

profit   Any gain; the amount of money gained after all the costs of a business are paid.

prop   Any article that can be moved which is not scenery or costumes and is used on a set of a theater.

publishing company   A business which produces and offers printed materials, such as books, for sale to the public.

radar   A device for locating and tracking objects by sending out radio waves and observing how and from where they are reflected.

research   The carefully organized study of a subject.

service   Useful work done, usually for the good of the general public, such as road building or police protection.

skewer   A long wooden or metal pin used to hold meat together while it is roasting or broiling.

skill   An ability to do something, resulting from practice and training.

sound effect   A sound that is artificially produced to imitate a sound, such as thunder or rain.

stage   A raised platform on which actors and actresses perform.

supervisor   The person in charge of and directing other employees.

123456789   BP   Printed in Canada   432109876

BEACH SCHOOL LIBRARY
1710 N. HUMBOLDT
PORTLAND, OREGON 97217

DATE DUE